300 THINGS TO DRAW

CREATIVE PROMPTS TO INSPIRE YOUR INNER ARTIST

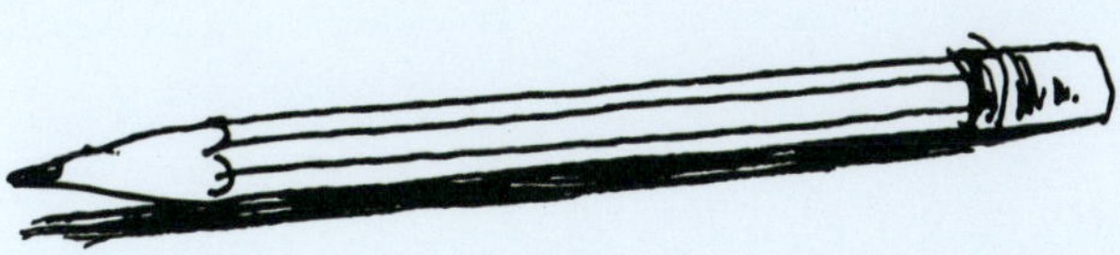

300 THINGS TO DRAW

CREATIVE PROMPTS TO INSPIRE YOUR INNER ARTIST

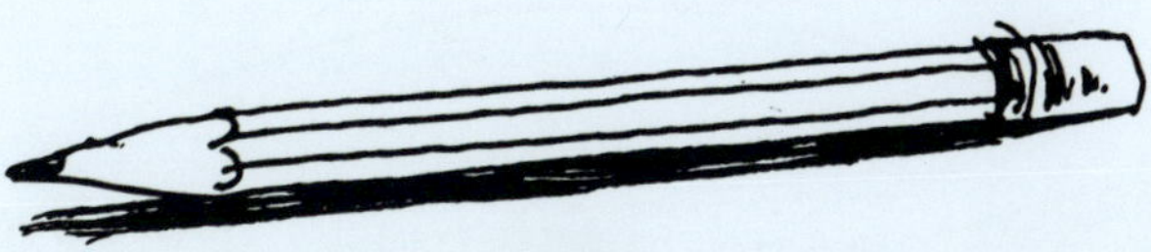

chartwell
books

KICK START YOUR CREATIVITY!

Sometimes all you need to get started is a nudge in the right direction, especially when you're trying to create something. Once you take the first step, you're on your way.

These 300 drawing ideas are designed to offer a creative lens on everyday life and a window into the world beyond your view. From the mundane to the whimsical, these ideas set you on a creative journey that will test your skills even as it expands them.

Whether you're an experienced artist looking to challenge yourself or a novice wanting to develop your artistic ability, the drawing prompts in this book offer a range of opportunities to try something new or hone your talent.

Flip through the pages and find a drawing idea that inspires you. Pursue it, refine it, and finish it before moving on to the next. Or draw a quick sketch and let it sit until you get further inspiration. Everything you try helps you to become a better artist!

Drawing offers something for everyone. You never know where these exercises in creativity will take you. Take the first step by trying and you're on your way to a more artistic you!

Happy drawing!

1. A Dolphin

2. Sunflowers

3. City Skyline

4. A Tortoise

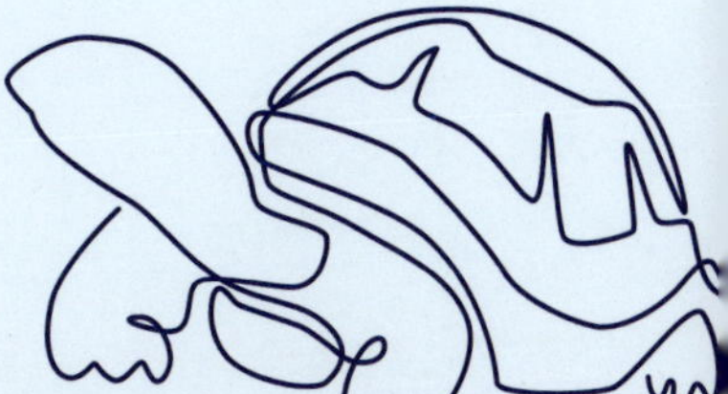

5. A Seahorse

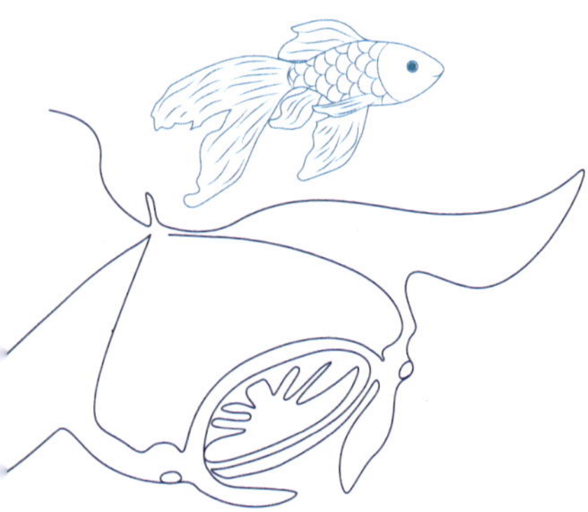

6. A Gardener at Work

7. A Pair of High-Heeled Shoes

8. A Swan

9. A Wasp or Bee

10. A Honeycomb

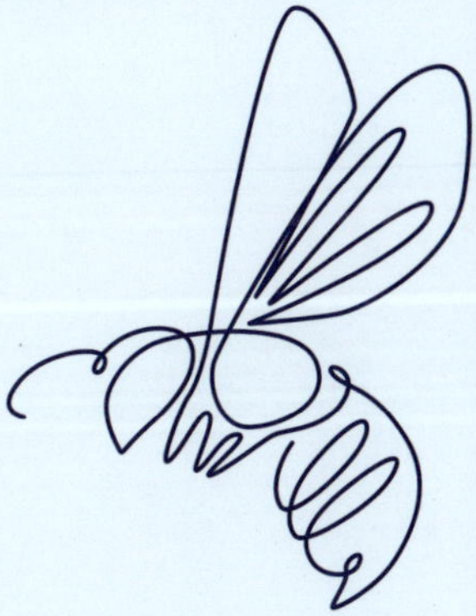

11. A Shipwreck

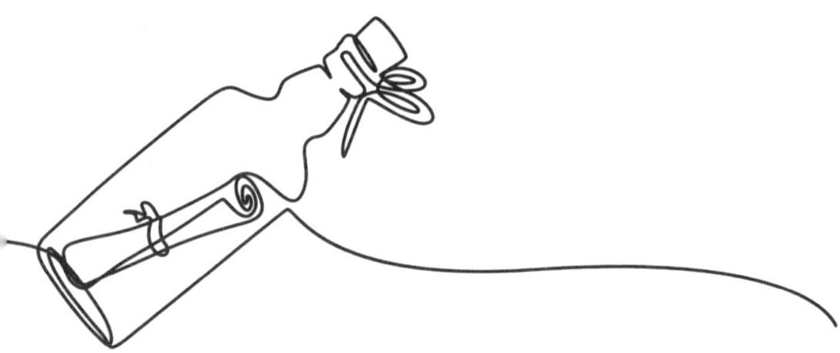

12. A Fox

13. A Lighthouse

14. A Path of Moonlight on Water

15. Something on the Table in Front of You

16. A Tabby Cat

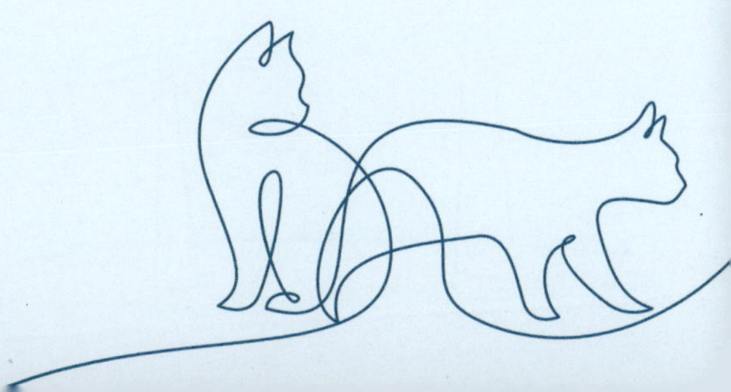

17. A Windmill

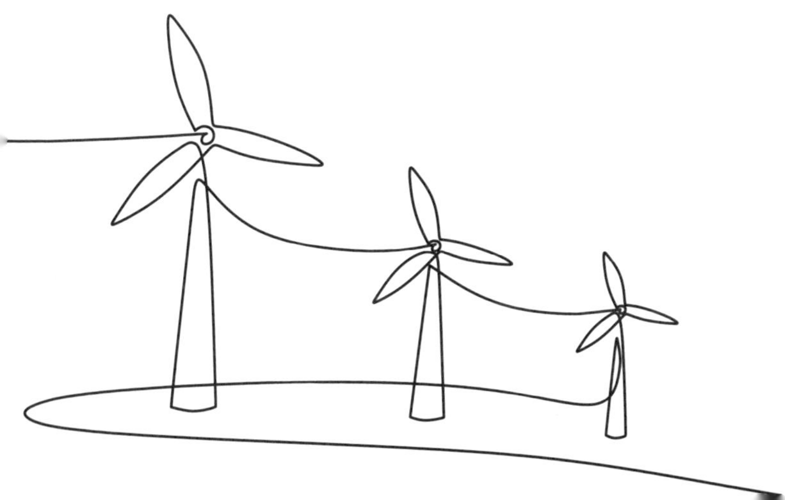

18. A Wolf Pack

19. A Jackrabbit

20. A Mermaid

21. A Snowman

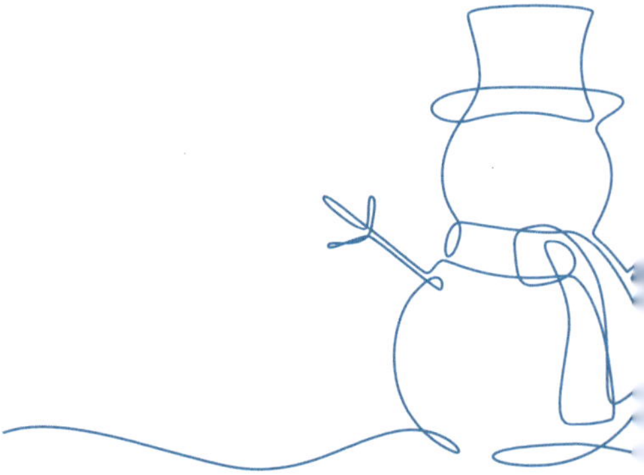

22. A Fawn in the Forest

23. A Vase of Flowers

24. A Monkey

25. A Spring Day in a Garden

26. A Disco Ball

27. A Bookshelf Full of Books

28. A Pair of Glasses

29. Bubbles

30. A Flag Waving in the Wind

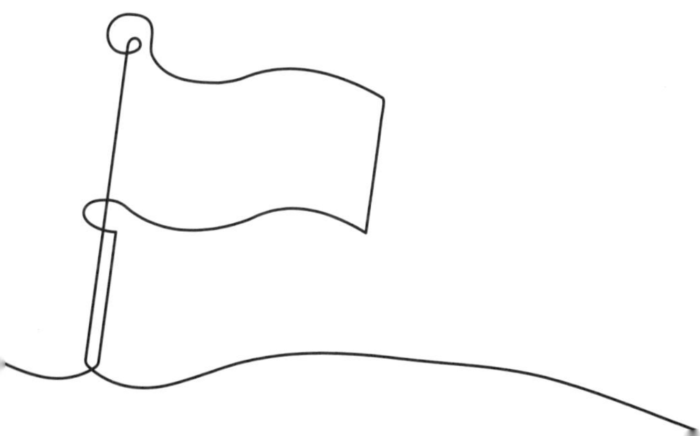

31. A Rainy Day Street Scene

32. A Claw-foot Tub

33. A Dancer

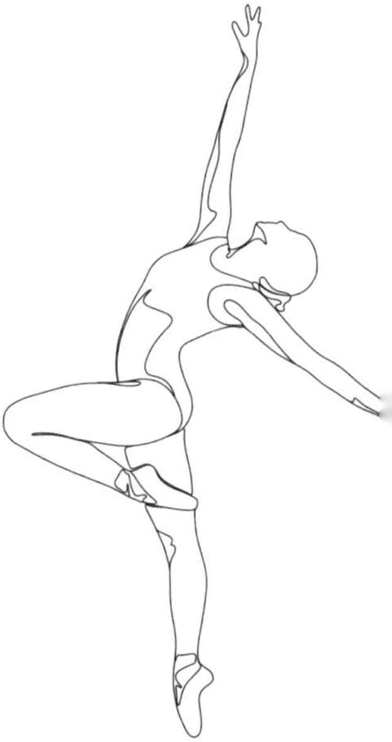

4. A Cafe Scene

35. A Bonfire

36. A Campfire Scene

37. A UFO

38. A Cow

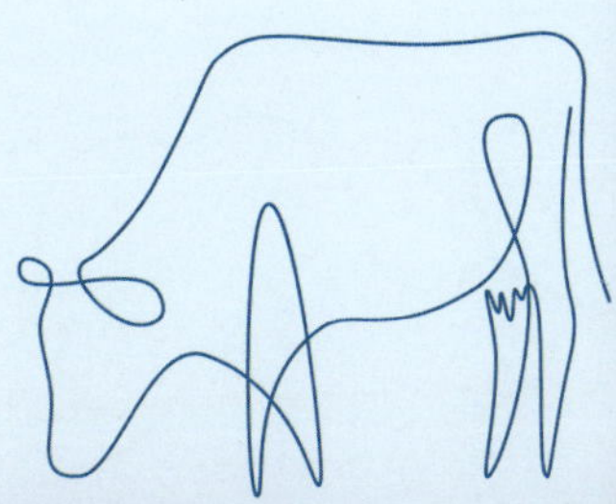

39. A Moustache

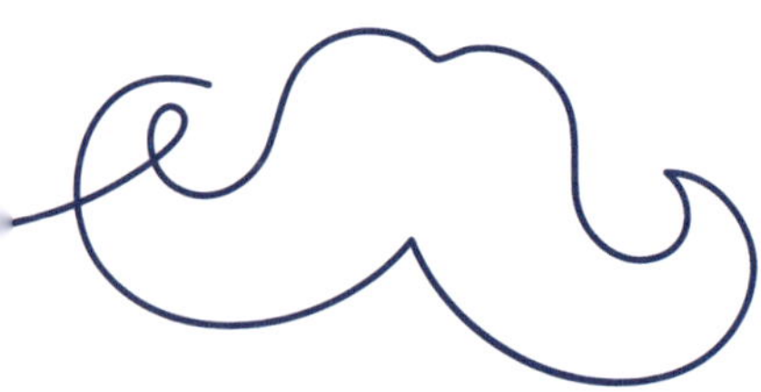

40. A Still Life with Fruit

41. A Halloween Costume

42. An Orchid

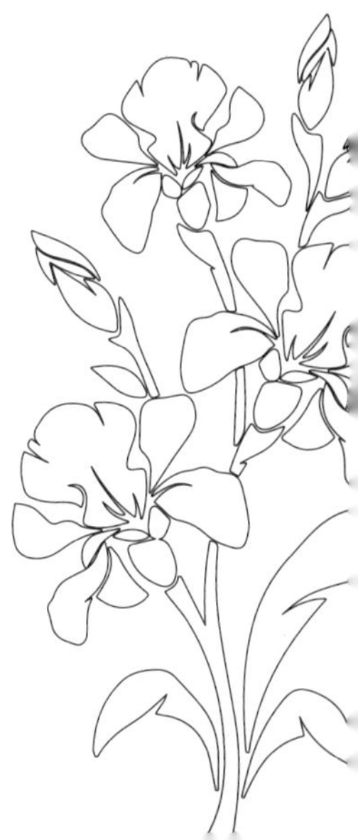

43. A Decorated Christmas Tree

44. A Moose

45. A Birthday Cake

46. A Lounge Chair

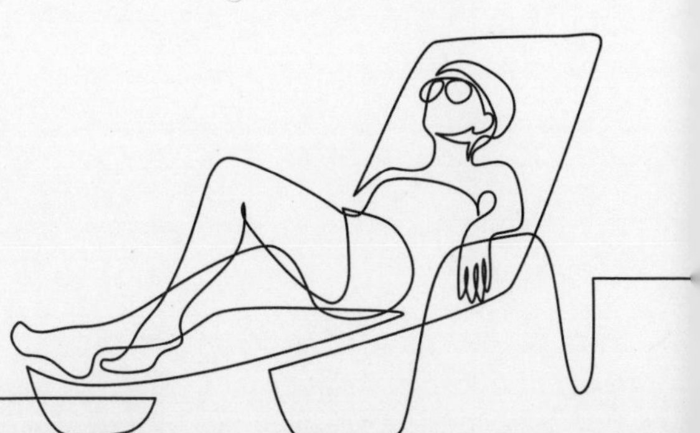

47. Shattered Glass

48. A Spider Web

49. A Puppy

50. A Fragment of Lace

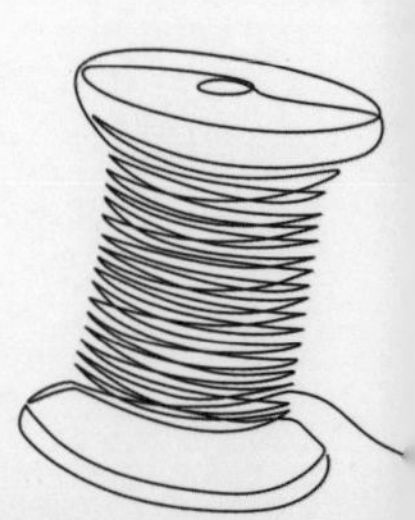

51. The Front Door of a House

52. A Cup of Tea

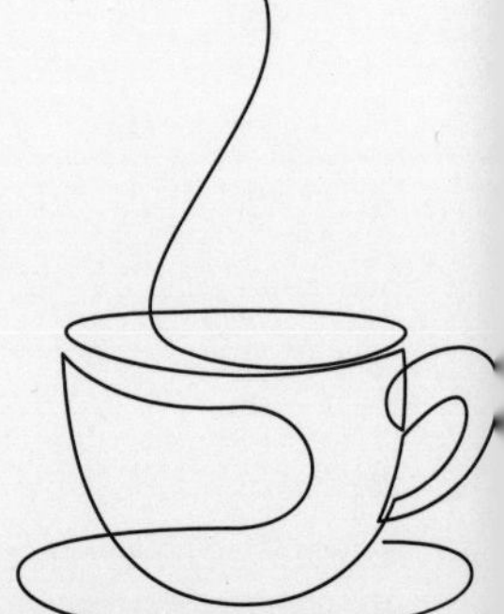

53. Horns or Antlers

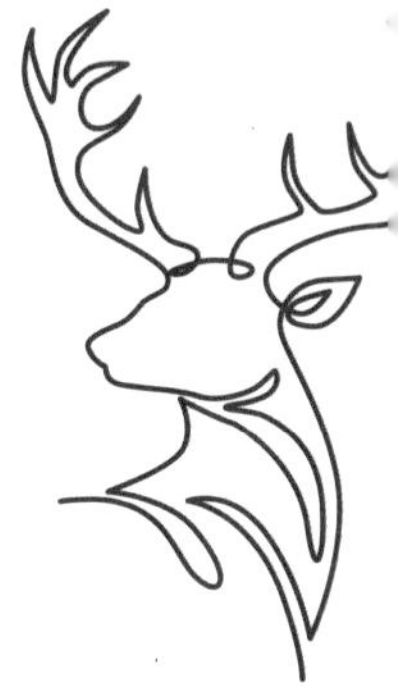

54. Salt & Pepper Shakers

55. A Wooden Fence

56. A Bear Cub

57. A Fishing Boat

58. A Dinner Scene

59. A Self Portrait

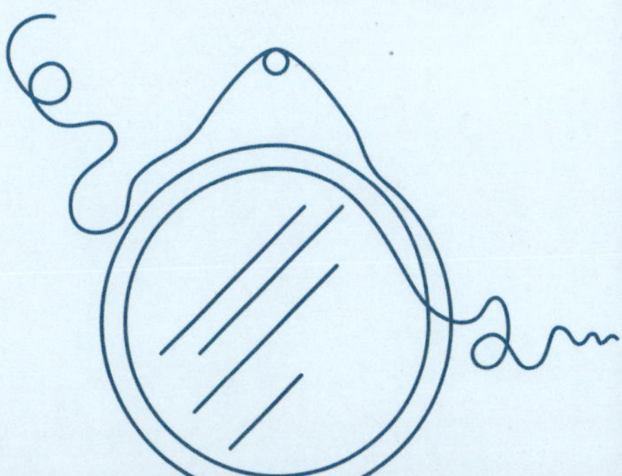

60. A Balloon Animal

61. A Weeping Willow Tree

62. A Clown

63. Fireworks

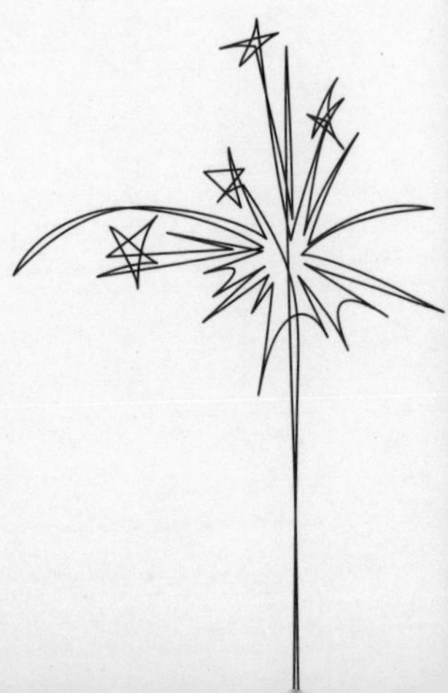

64. A Basket of Fruit

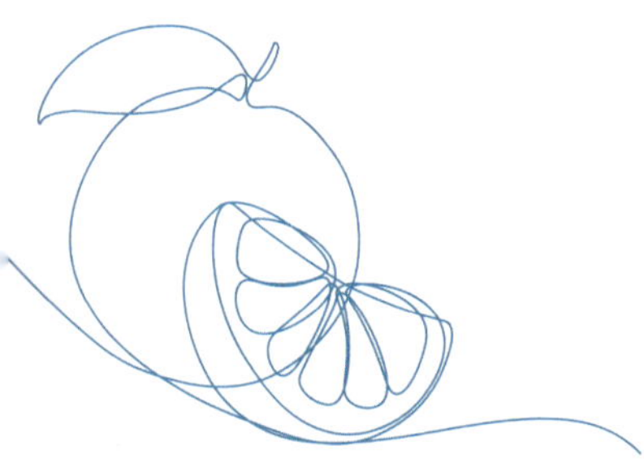

5. A Cartoon Character

66. Train Tracks

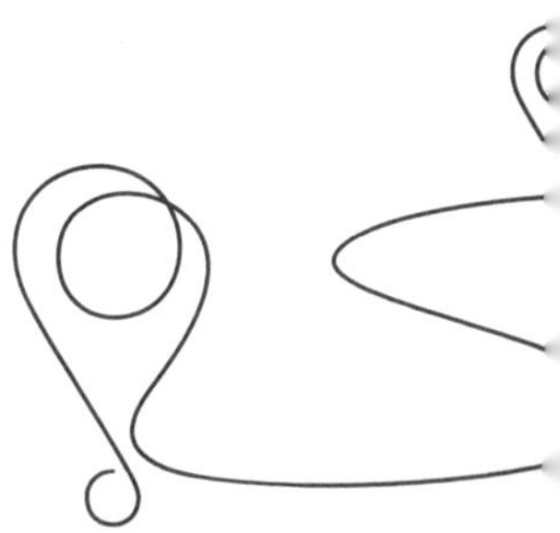

7. A Pear Tree

8. A Jack 'o' Lantern

69. A Farm Scene

70. A Fish Tank

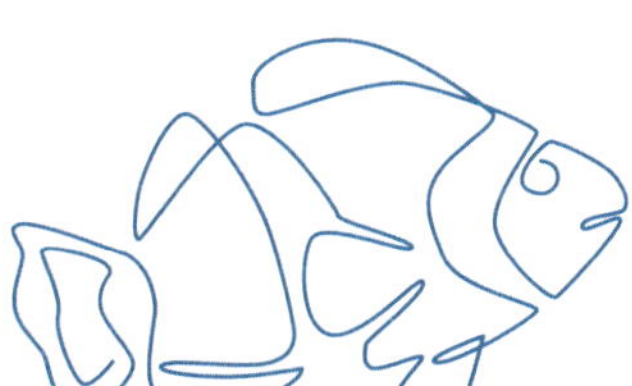

71. A Person Sleeping

72. A Religous Building

73. An Antique Camera

74. An Elephant

75. The Symbol for Your Zodiac Sign

76. A Bejeweled Crown

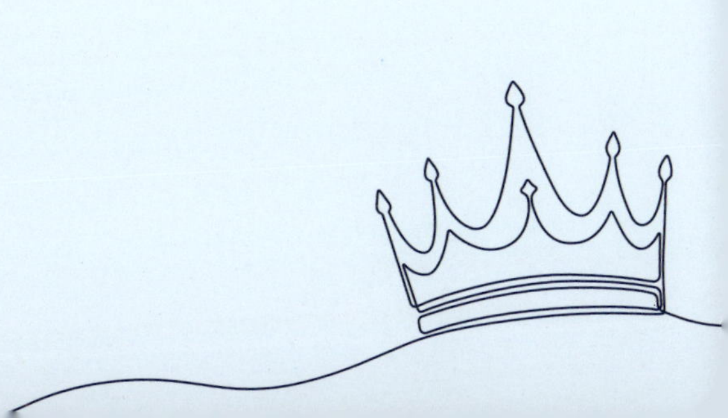

77. An Angel

78. A Ceremonial Mask

79. An Actor on Stage

80. A Work Desk

1. A Knight

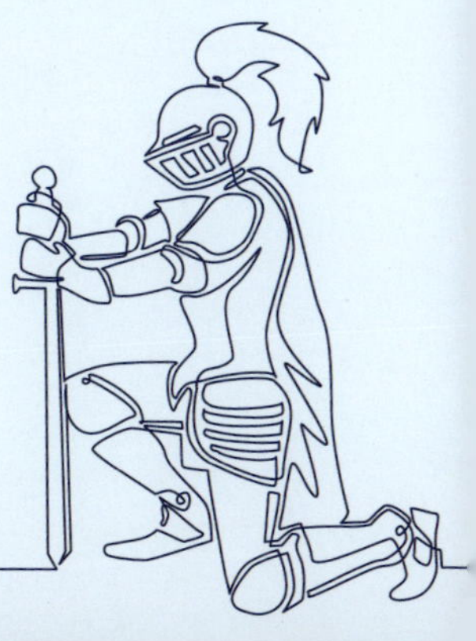

82. A Gate

83. A Surfboard

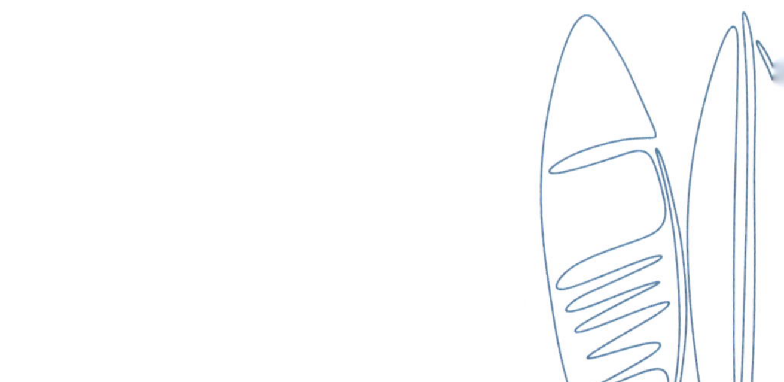

34. A Wine Bottle

35. A Typewriter

86. Graffiti

37. A Toucan

38. Puzzle Pieces

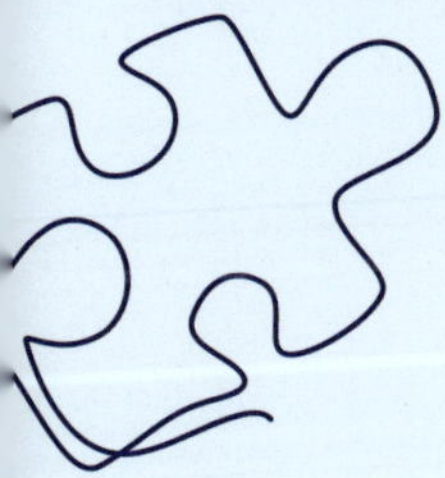

89. A Watermelon

90. A Penguin

1. A Bunch of Grapes

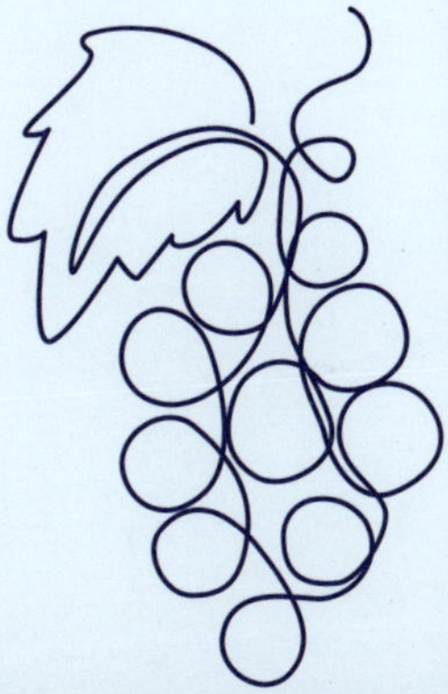

92. A Vampire

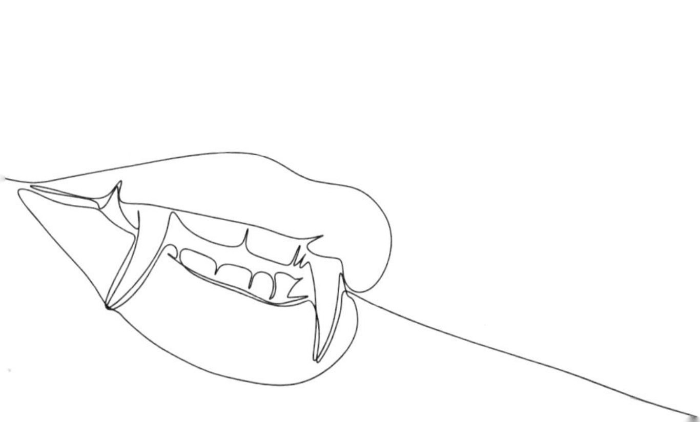

3. A Holiday Scene

4. A Weapon

95. A Tuba

96. A Fairy

7. Mushrooms

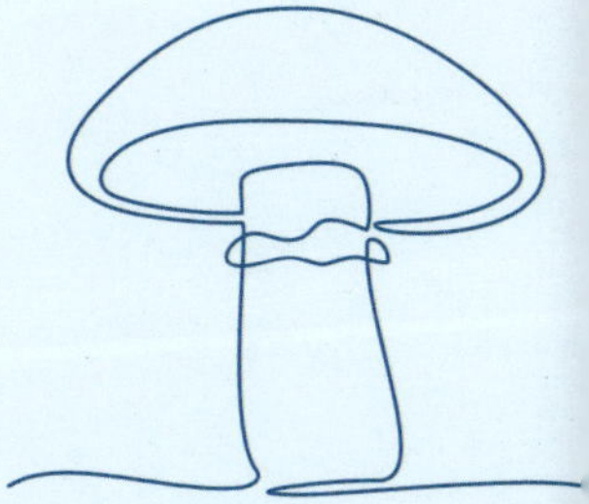

8. A City on a Hill

99. A Pair of Boots

100. A Buffet Dinner

01. An Open Window

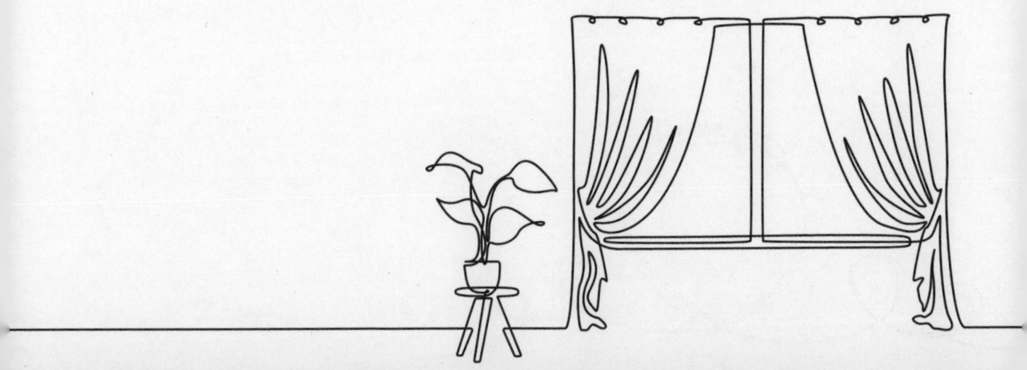

102. A Roller Coaster

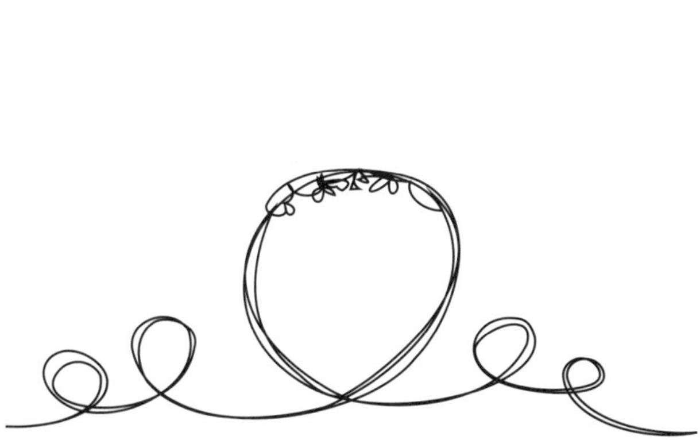

03. A Skeleton

104. A Chandelier

105. A Merry Go Round

106. A Sofa

107. An Artichoke

108. A Runner

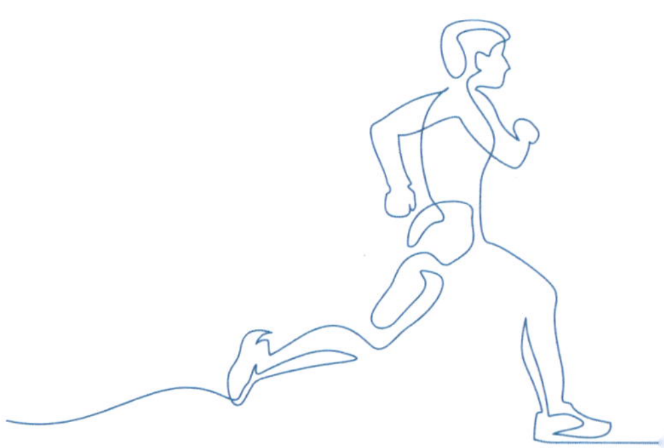

109. A Sporting Event

110. A Pizza

111. A Festival

112. A Sleeping Dog

13. An Ancient Ruin or Shrine

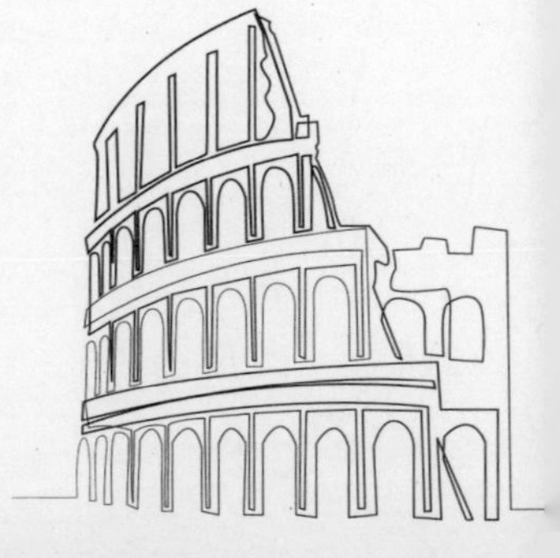

114. An Artist's Easel

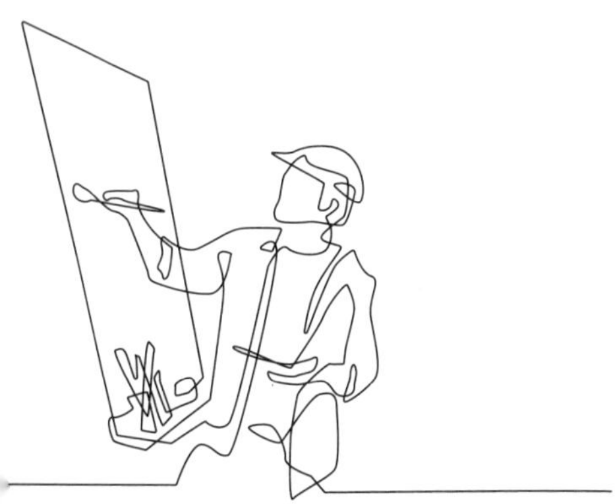

15. Dinner on the Stove

16. A Pretzel

117. A Piano

118. A Truck

19. A Propeller Plane

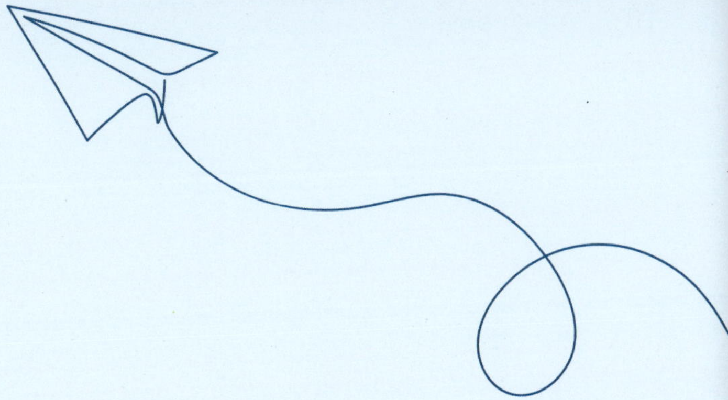

120. A Unicorn

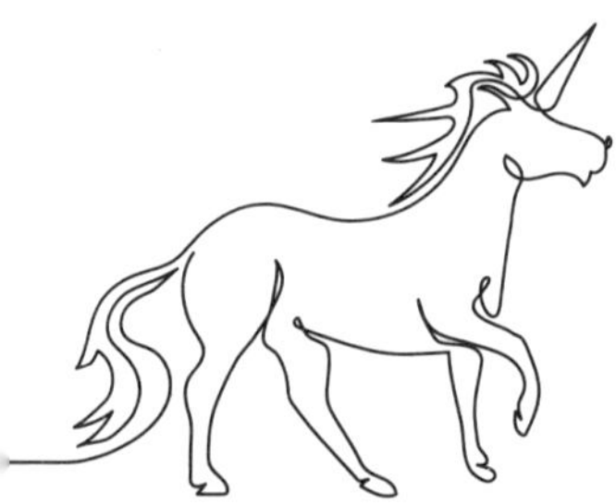

21. A Hot Air Balloon

122. A Peacock

123. A Doll

24. A Bowl of Soup

25. A Snowy Day

126. A Witch

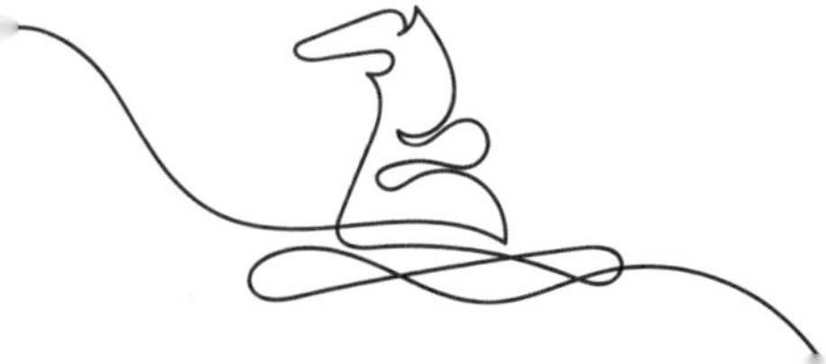

127. Pyramids

128. Pebbles

129. A Group of Friends

130. Waves

31. A Waterfall

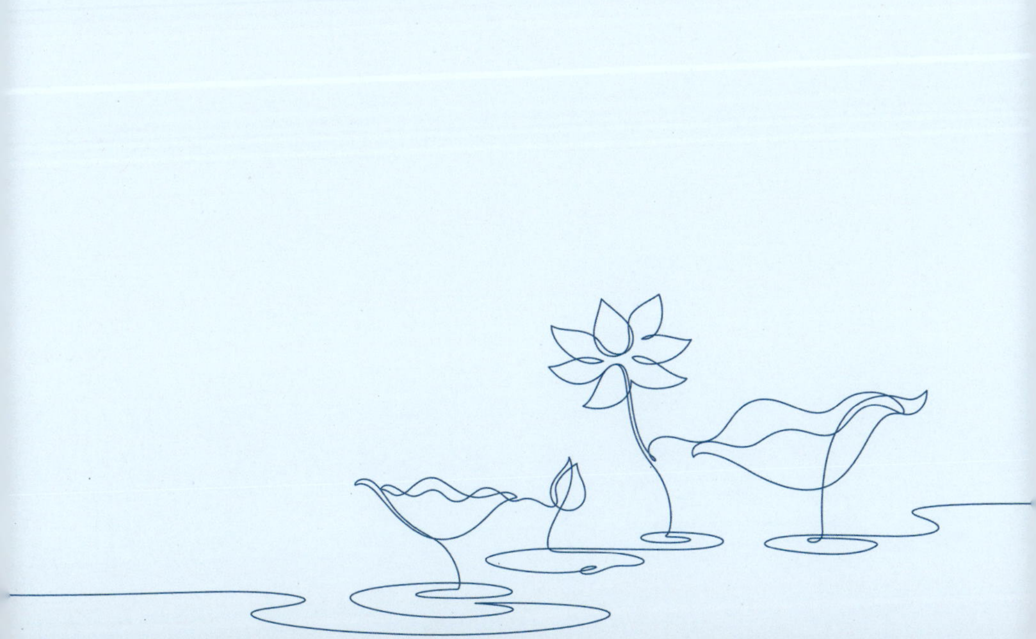

132. A Llama

133. A Sailboat

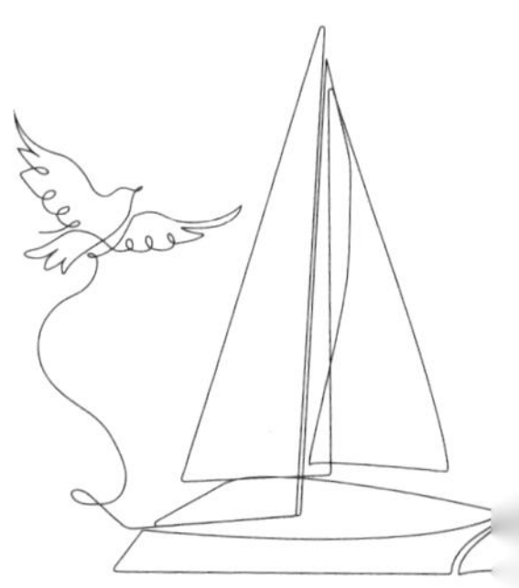

134. A Candle

135. A Skull

136. A Home

137. A Couple

38. A Castle

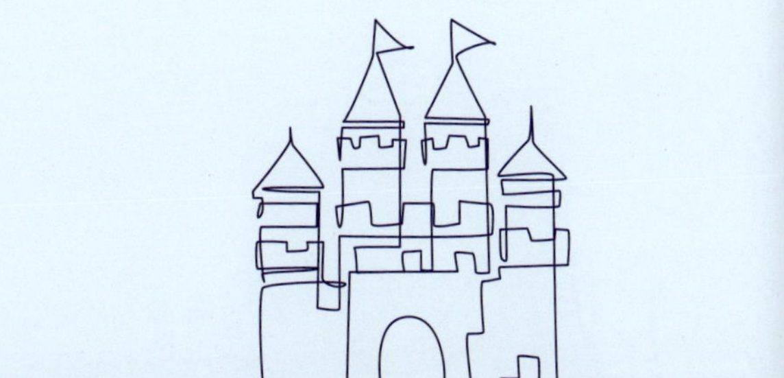

139. A Dinosaur

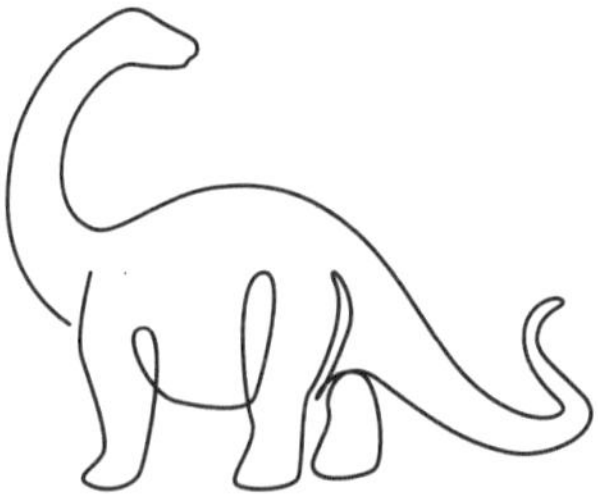

40. A Mountain

41. A Monument

142. A Summer Day at the Beach

143. A Surfboard

44. A Storm

145. A Dragon

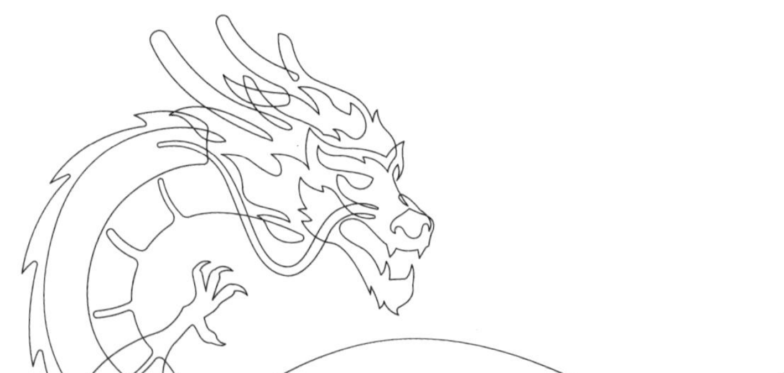

146. A Car

147. A Chicken

148. A Bridge

149. A Cowboy Hat

150. A Dinner Scene

151. A Garden Gnome

152. A Trophy

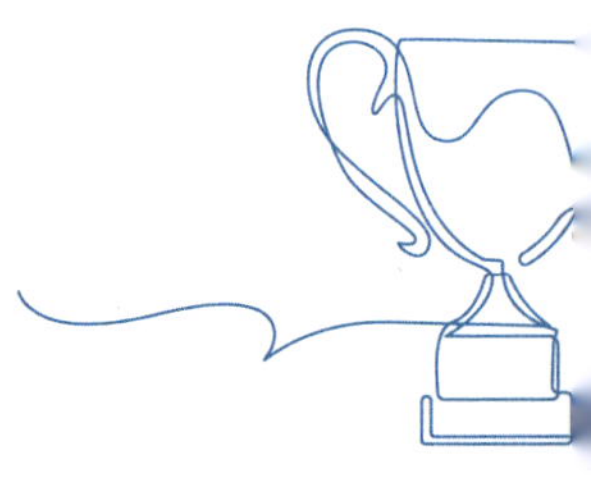

53. A Barrel

54. Someone Reading a Book

155. A Popcupine

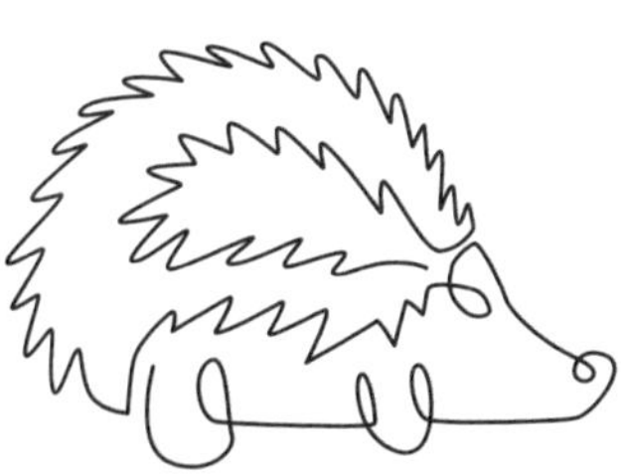

56. A Monster

157. A Goddess

58. Wings

159. A Climbing Vine

160. Postcards

61. A Cactus

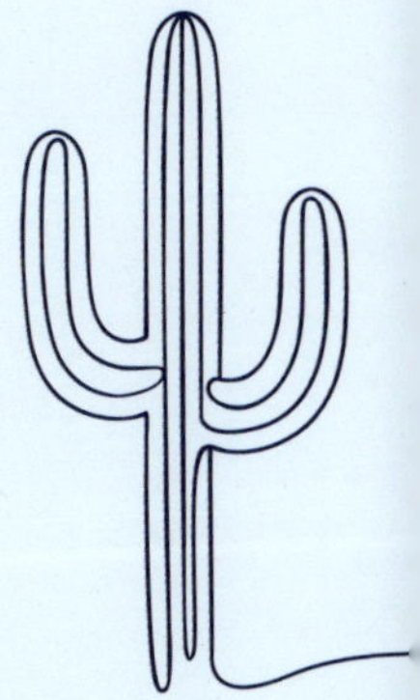

62. A Suitcase

163. A Pirate

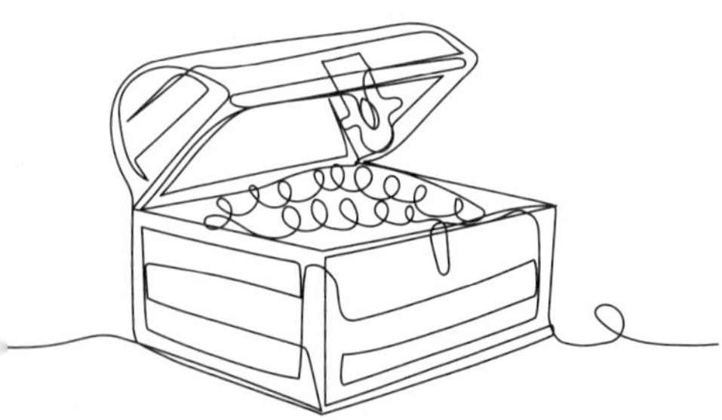

64. A Holiday Wreath

65. A Kangaroo

166. A Feather

167. A Horse

68. A Beach Scene

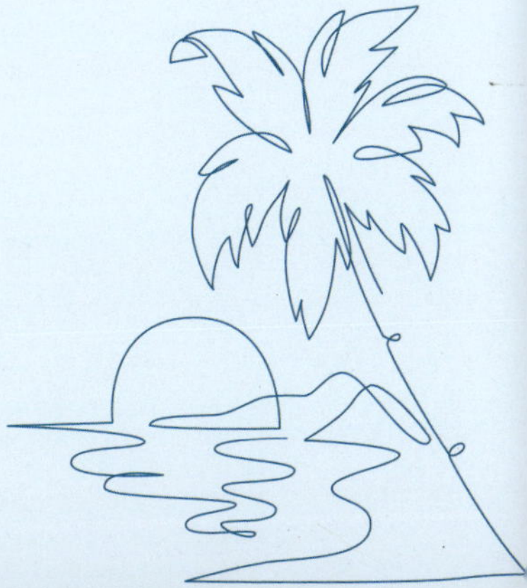

169. A Jellyfish

170. A Koi Pond

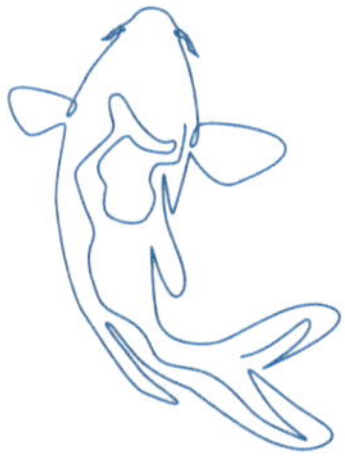

71. Clouds

72. A View from A Mountaintop

173. A Praying Mantis

174. A Leaf Falling from a Tree

75. A Ghost

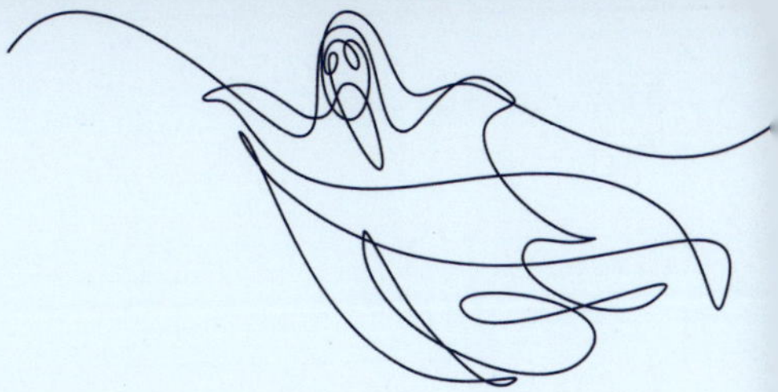

176. A Throne

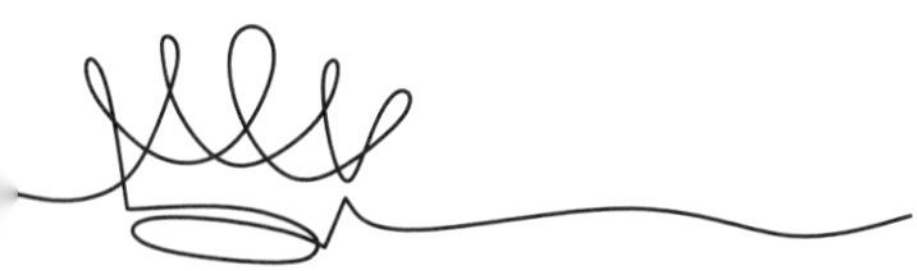

77. A Meadow

78. A Narwhal

179. A Toolbox

180. An Artist at Work

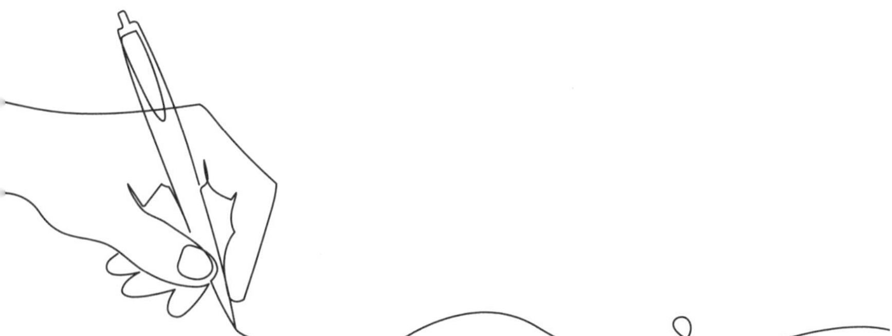

81. Students in a Ballet Studio

82. An Empty Street

183. A Treehouse

84. A Child Playing

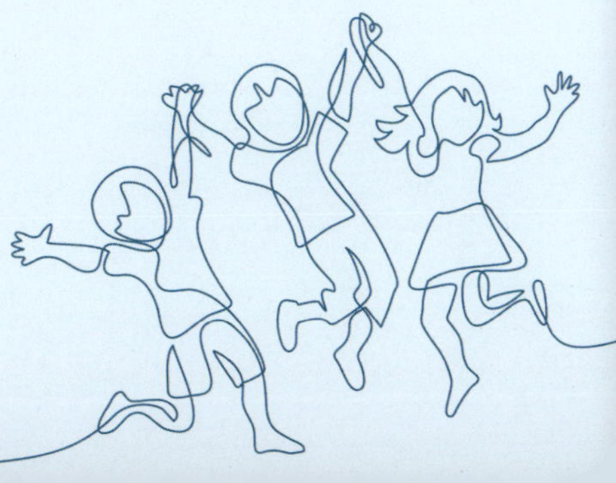

185. A Lobster

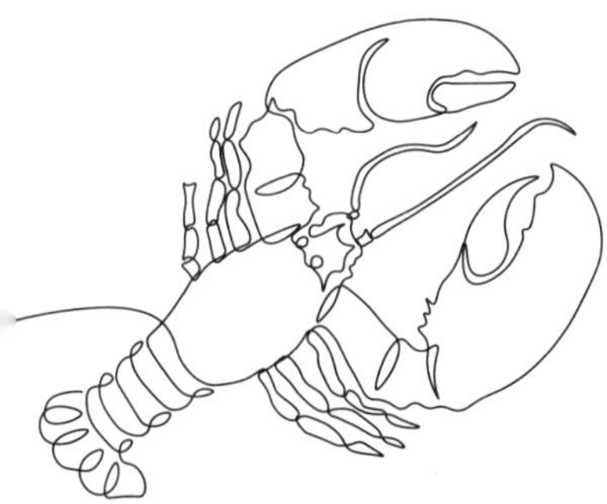

86. A Bicycle

87. A Chessboard

188. A Jar with the Lid Off

189. A Kitchen Table

90. A Warrior

91. A Winter Hat and Scarf

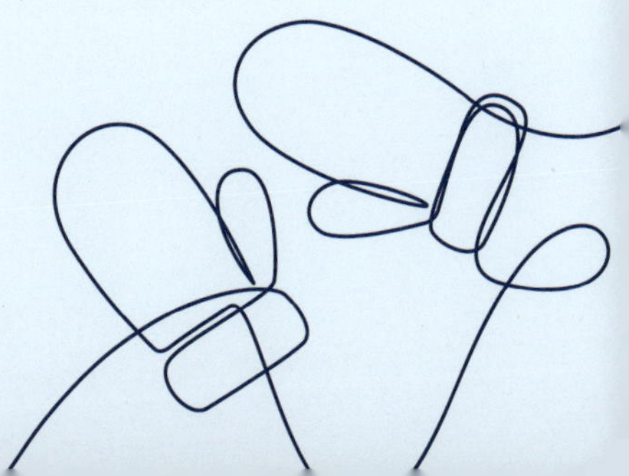

192. A Musical Instrument

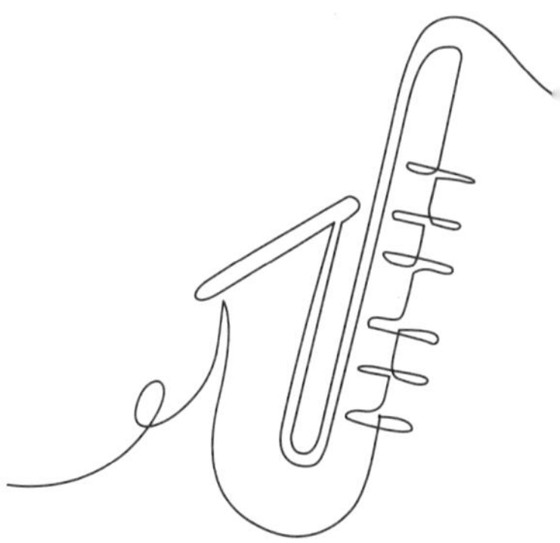

93. A Child's Toy

194. A Haystack

195. A Picnic

96. An Alligator

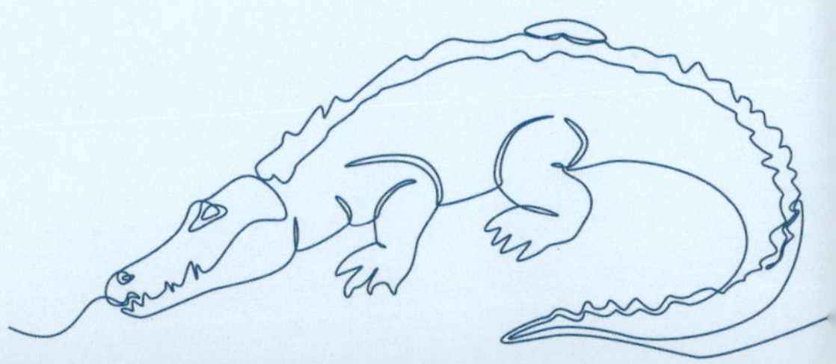

197. A Pitcher of Water

198. A Dive into A Pool

99. A Smile

200. A Potted Plant

201. A Scene from a Parade

202. A Frog

203. A Giraffe

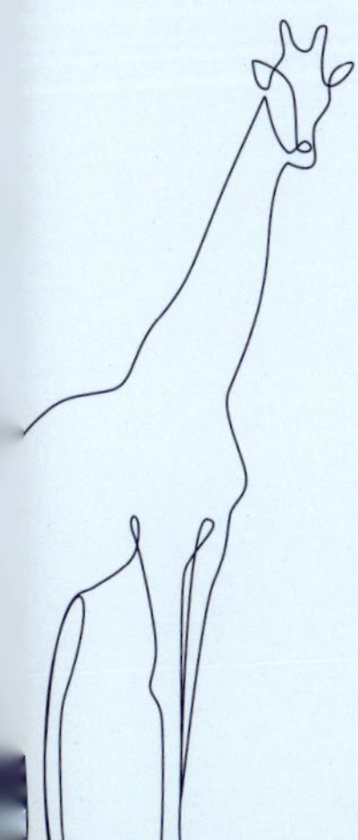

204. An Alien Creature

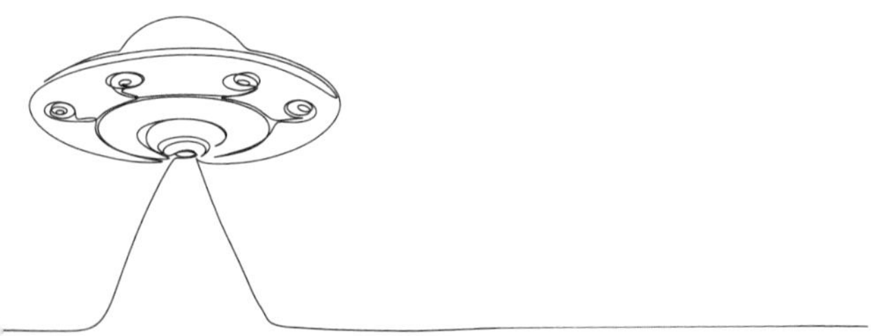

205. A Store Window

206. A Stairway

207. A Knit Sweater

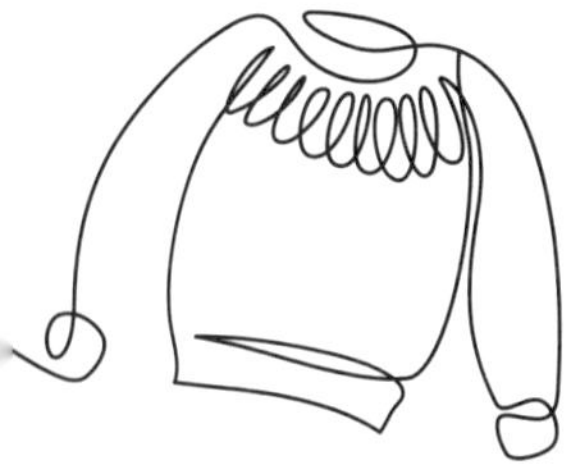

208. A Stack of Dishes

209. A Birdcage

210. A Wine Glass

211. A Loaf of Bread

212. A Snake Poised to Strike

13. Footprints

15. A Volcanic Explosion

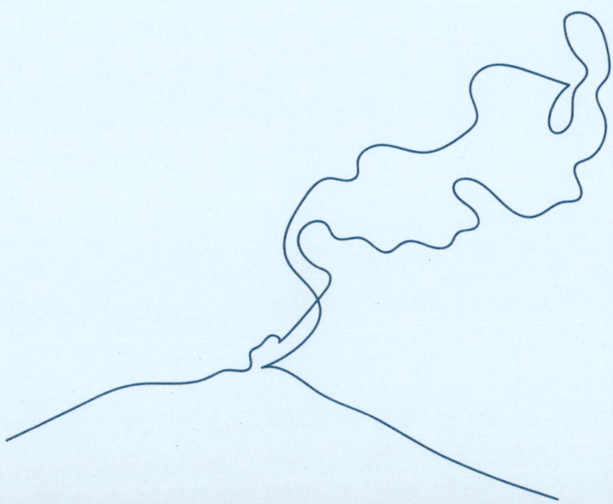

216. A Face in Profile

217. A Tree Bent in the Wind

18. A Seashell

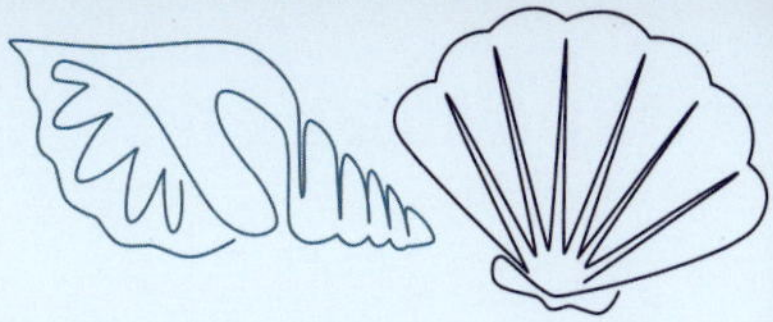

. . . .

19. A Coffee Pot

220. A Puppet

221. A Garden Arbor

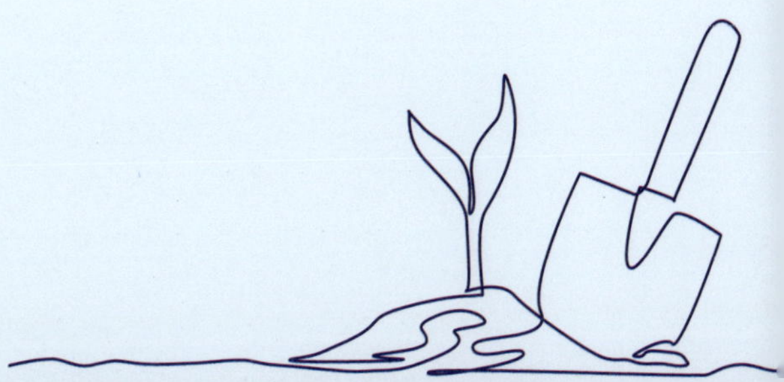

222. A Zombie

223. A Pair of Hands

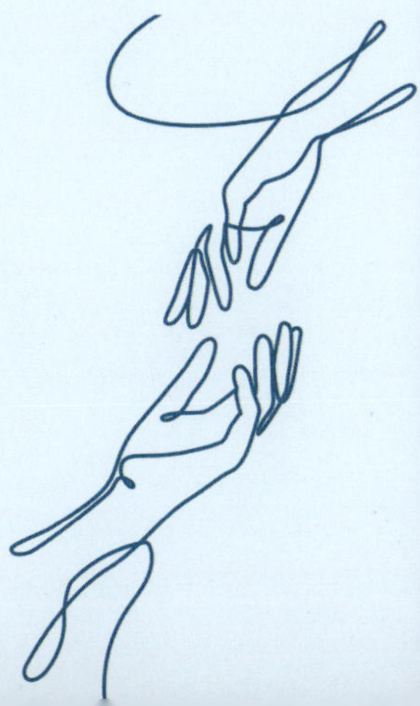

224. A Raven

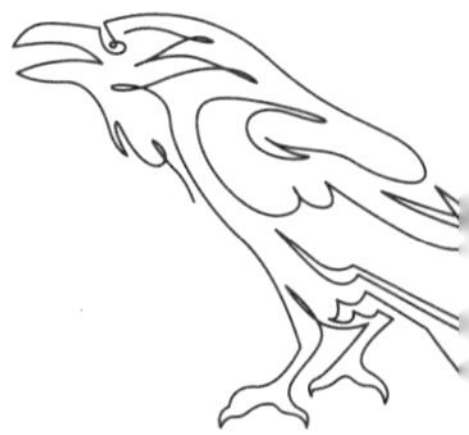

225. A Set of Claws

226. A Pair of Eyes

227. A Graveyard

228. A Sloth

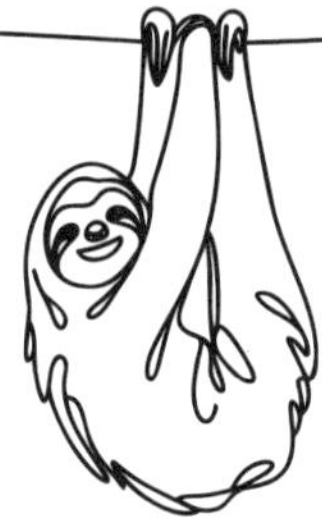

229. A Card Game

230. A Pomegranate

231. An Owl

232. A Lantern

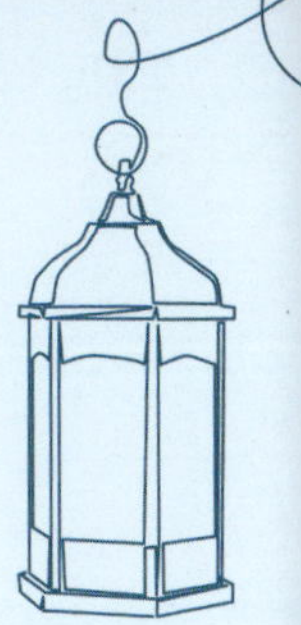

233. A Ball Gown

234. A Bird's Nest

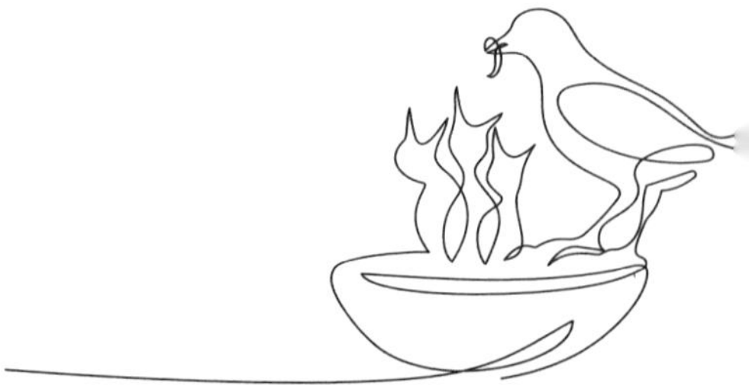

35. A Fan

36. A Stack of Laundry

237. A Treasure Chest

238. A Set of Keys

239. Dunes at a Beach

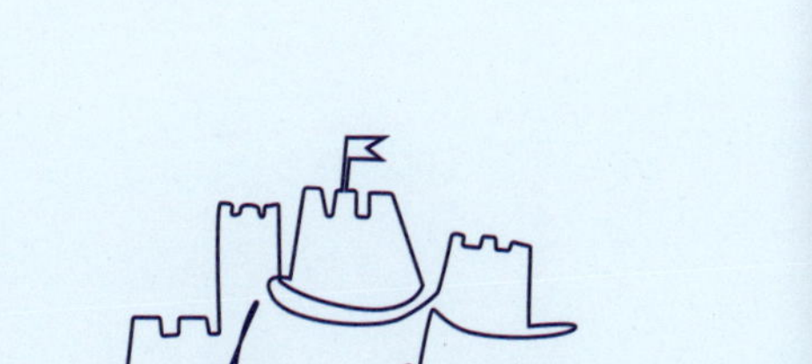

240. A Tower

241. A Swing Set

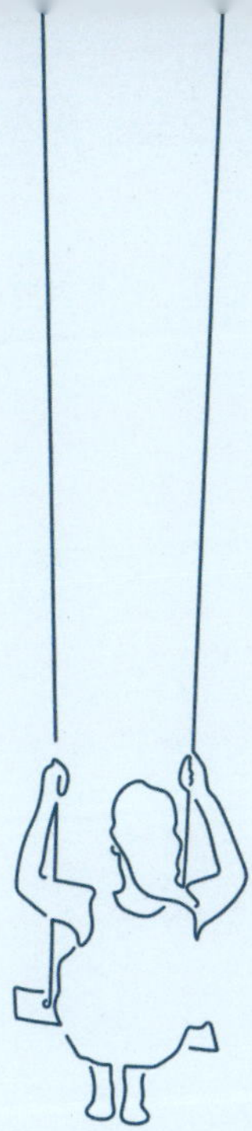

242. Icicles

243. A Skating Scene

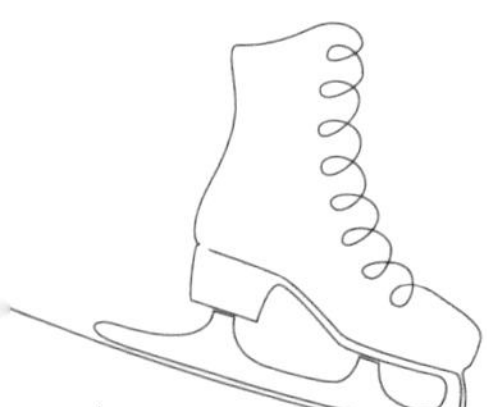

44. A Snail

45. A Streetlight

246. A Dressmaker's Model

47. A Pond

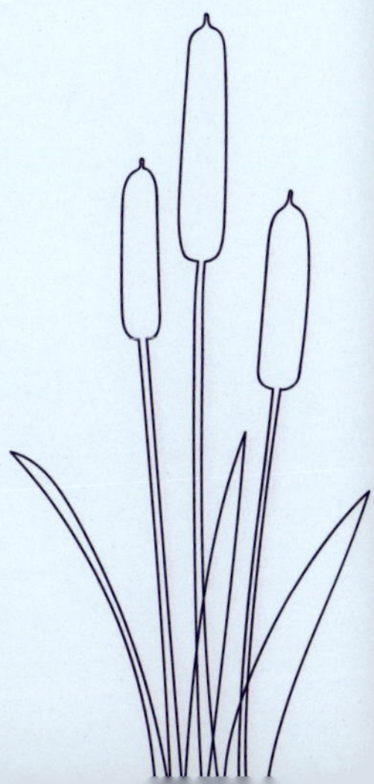

248. A Classical Statue

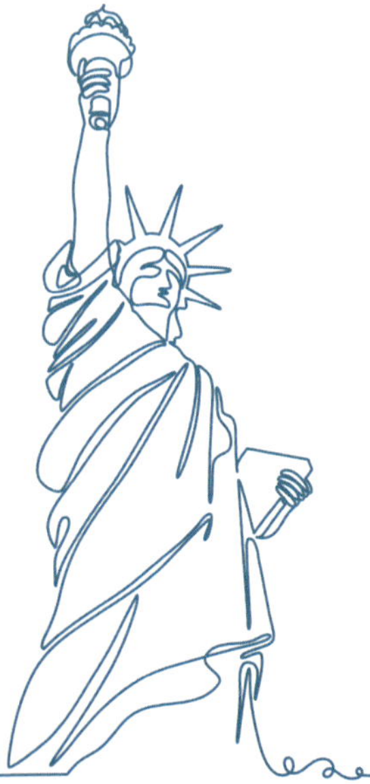

249. A Scarecrow

250. An Artist's Palette

251. A Plush Toy

52. A Street Market

53. A Cafe Scene

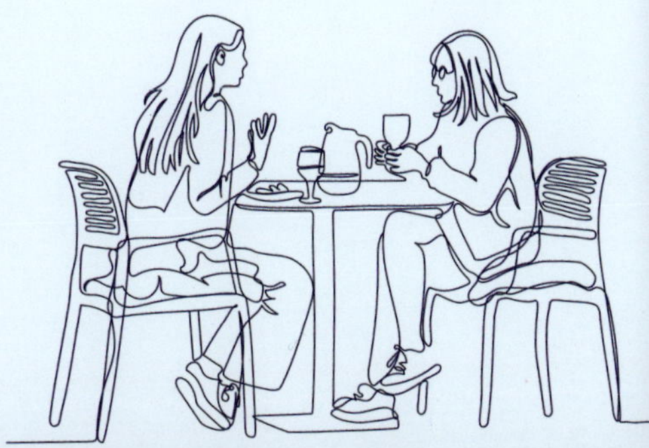

254. A Bonsai Tree

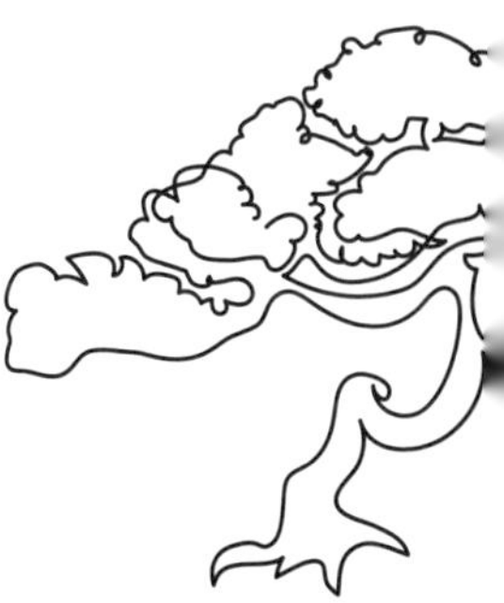

255. A Bat

256. A Seal

257. A Fountain

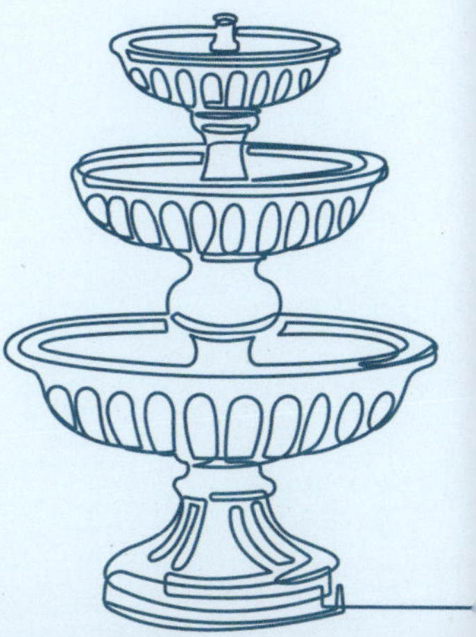

258. A Water Bottle

59. A Backpack

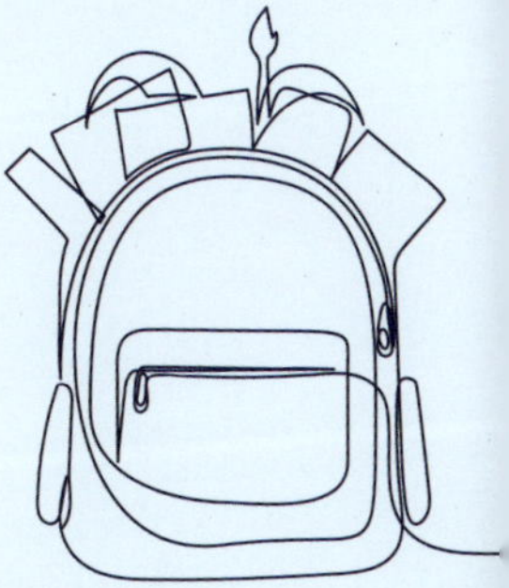

60. An Avocado

261. A Cliff

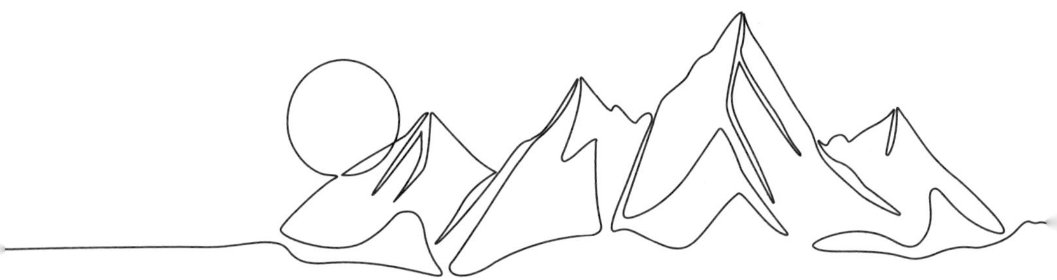

62. A Lock

263. A Box of Chocolates

264. A Rat

265. A Street Peformer

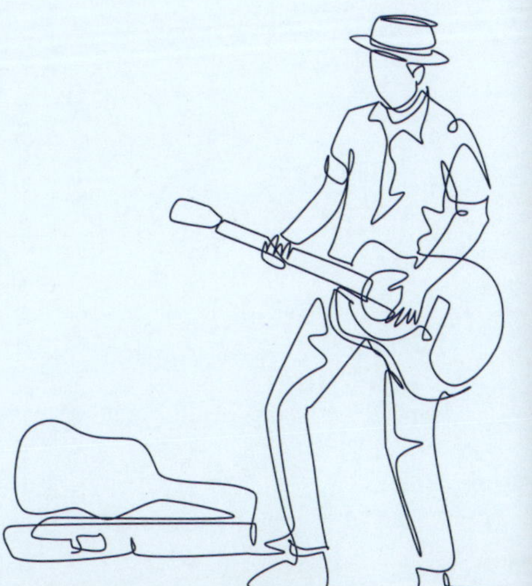

266. A Movie Marquee

267. A Ladder

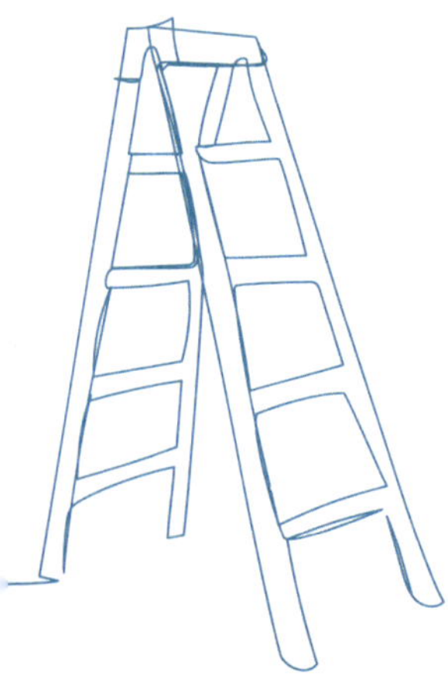

268. A Champagne Bottle

269. An Armchair

270. A Red Carpet Entrance

271. The Moon & Stars

272. A Baby

273. A Circus Performer

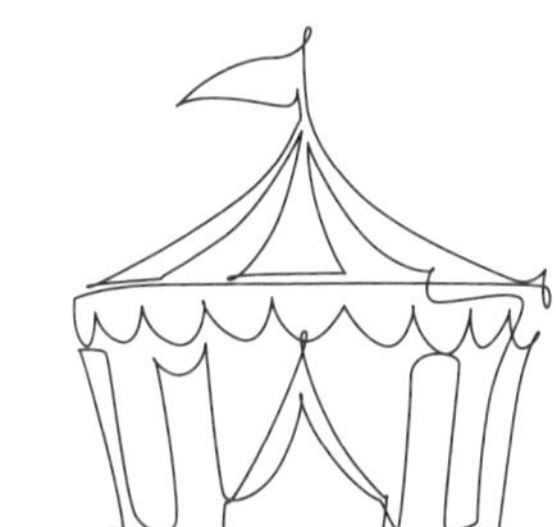

274. Orange Slices

275. A Piece of Cake

276. A Lilypad

77. A Full Shopping Bag

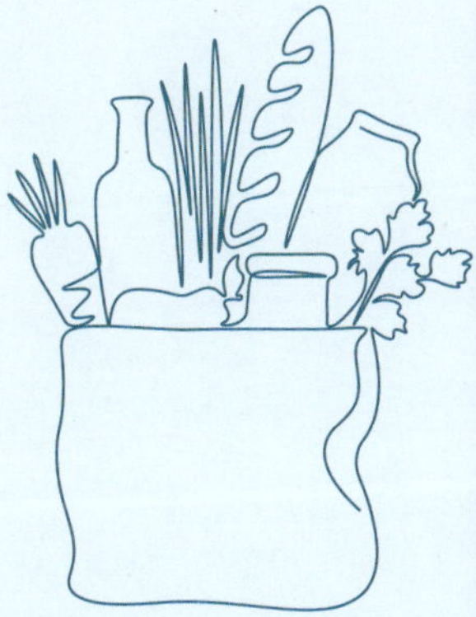

78. A Sleeping Kitten

279. An Accordian

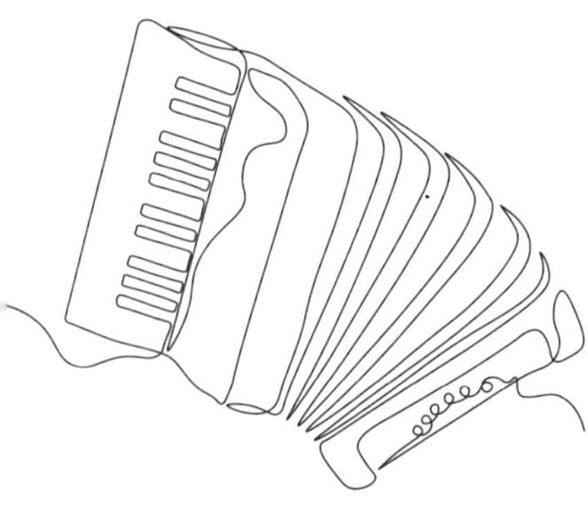

280. A Palm Tree

281. A Tunnel

282. An Unmade Bed

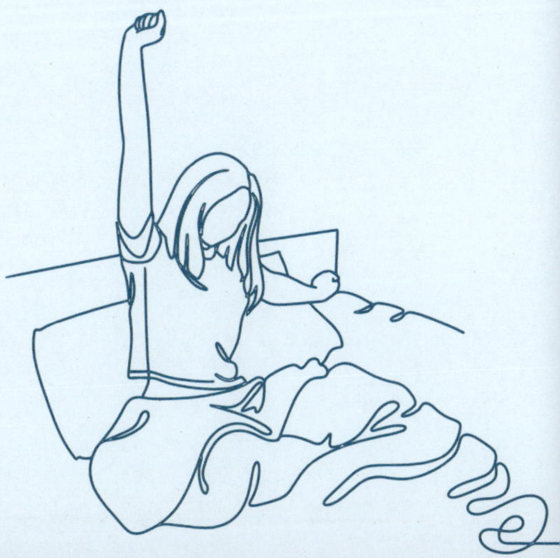

283. A Windy Day

284. A Compass

285. A Guitar

286. A Wedding

287. A Pinecone

288. A Tree Stump

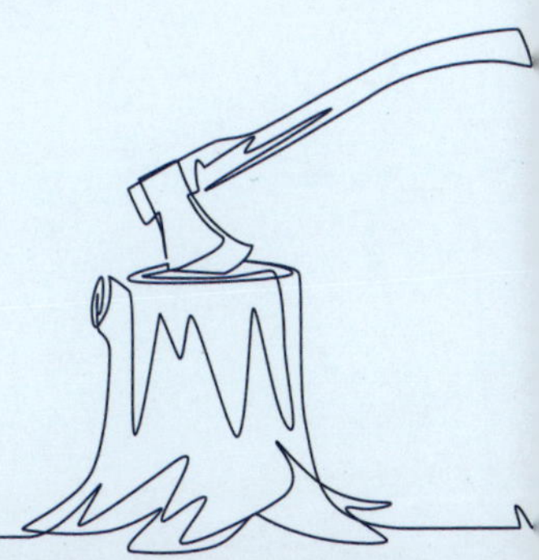

289. A Dessert

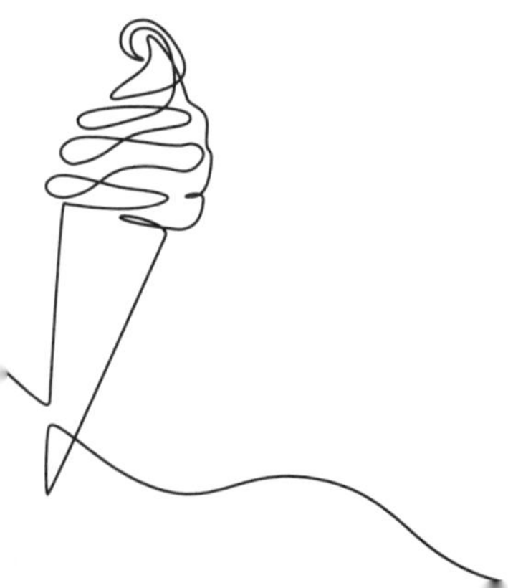

290. A Snowflake

291. A Tragedy

292. An Arguement

293. A Sheep

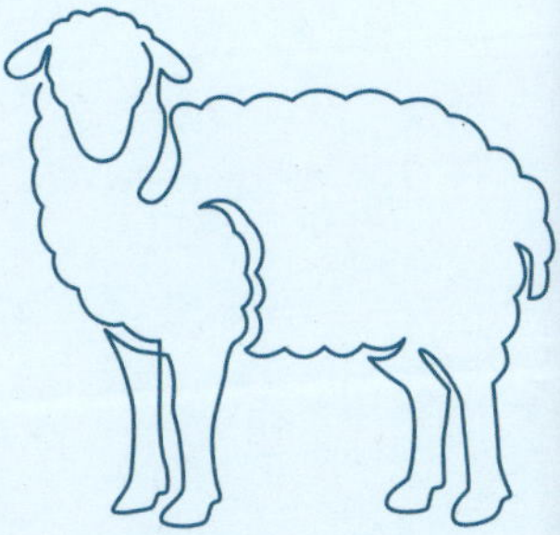

294. A Camper Van

295. A Barn

296. A Sunrise or Sunset

297. Curtains Fluttering in the Breeze

298. A Leaf

299. A Streetlight

300. A Bird Eye's View

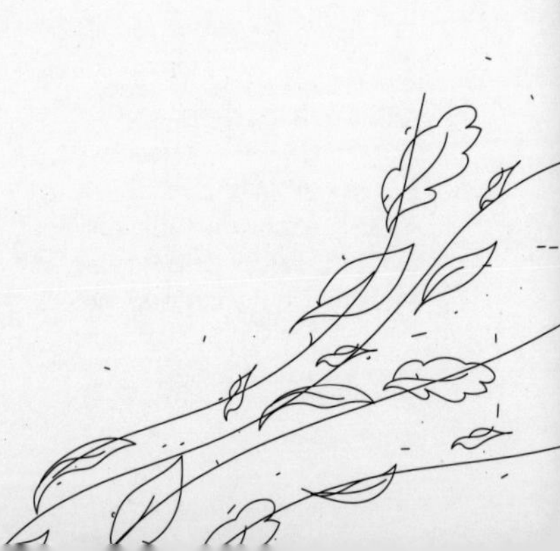

Quarto

This edition published in 2025 by Chartwell Books,
an imprint of The Quarto Group,
142 West 36th Street, 4th Floor,
New York, NY 10018, USA
T (212) 779-4972
www.Quarto.com

Previously published in 2020 by Chartwell Books, an imprint of The Quarto Group, 142 West 36th Street, 4th Floor, New York, NY 10018, USA

10 9 8 7 6 5 4 3 2 1

ISBN: 978-0-7858-4663-5

Publisher: Wendy Friedman
Editor: Joanne O'Sullivan
Cover Design: Sue Boylan
Interior Design: Alana Ward

Printed in Malaysia